Critters Galore Outside Your Door

by **Kirk Eason**

Critters Galore Outside Your Door

Where do you look for critters galore?
They're right outside your own back door.
They live free of fences, no bars like a zoo.
You're watching them, they're watching you!

The sad little CATERPILLAR has reason to cry.
She moves so slowly and knows she can't fly.
A cocoon she will build and curl up inside.
With wings she'll emerge to fly off with pride.

Fun Facts:

The Monarch is the king of the BUTTERFLIES. It can fly over 2000 miles without getting lost. It's an amazing critter, that started out as a lowly CATERPILLAR.

A SQUIRREL you can't beat to the top of a tree.
A better climber there just can't be.
Sure of himself, he knows he won't fall.
He jumps limb to limb, he's the best of them all.

Fun Facts:

Guess who can run down
a tree trunk head first?

Yep, a SQUIRREL can. He's also
known for his ability to hide acorns
in the summer and fall, so he can
eat them on a frozen winter day.

The TURTLE moves slowly, but he's carrying his home:
A shell so hard you'd think it was stone.
When trouble approaches, and he can tell
He's safe and secure in his very own shell.

Fun Facts:

All kids love playing with TURTLES. They have a very hard shell, which gives great protection. Baby turtles hatch from eggs that are buried in the sand. The adults hunt for food during the day.

If you walk in the woods in the late day sun,
You might spot a critter that should make you run.
But suddenly you notice how much it stunk...
'Cause you've been sprayed by the smelly old SKUNK!

Fun Facts:

You probably won't believe it,
but SKUNKS often attack bee hives,
because they eat the bees. Not a
good idea! Skunks spray a horrible
smelling liquid, when threatened, that
will not go away for days.

He lives in the woods not far from your home.
When the sun goes down, the RACCOON will roam.
With a little black mask that crosses his face,
He'll steal all your garbage and mess up your place.

Fun Facts:

Who's the messiest of all the critters?
It must be the RACCOON,
because she is always eating
out of somebody's garbage.

A BUMBLEBEE'S jacket is striped black and gold.
He arrives in the summer 'cause he doesn't like cold.
His nectar he gets with his long lapping tongue.
Leave him alone, or you'll probably get stung.

Fun Facts:

BUMBLEBEES live in small nests
and do not swarm like other bees.
They are not very aggressive and
won't attack unless threatened.
They have four wings.

DOGS are the critters that we all know the best.
They'll do anything for us and play with no rest.
Their master is someone they'll always defend;
Because of their loyalty, they're "man's best friend."

Fun Facts:

The United States has the highest DOG population of anywhere in the world. Puppies sleep almost the entire day for the first 3 weeks. Dogs are best known for their keen sense of smell and their extra sharp hearing.

About the time when day turns to night,
A LIGHTNING BUG passes and flashes his light.
They're fun to catch and put in a jar,
Then let them loose and they'll shine like a star.

Fun Facts:

Did you know that LIGHTNING BUGS
talk to each other using light signals?
You could have fun doing this
with a friend.

A KITTEN so cute, oh how can it be?
I really want one to come live with me.
Their feet are padded and they're quiet as a mouse,
But mice would be smart to start leaving the house.

Fun Facts:

Guess what! KITTENS are the most popular pets in the world. They are excellent hunters and can see well at night. When falling from a height, they seem to always land on their feet.

I see a LADYBUG all dressed in red
With spots on her body and a little black head.
She eats the small bugs that kill the farm crop.
The farmer is happy and hopes she won't stop.

Fun Facts:

Aphids are very tiny insects that can
eat and kill some farm crops.
But guess who eats aphids?
Yep, a LADYBUG can eat as many
as 75 of the insects a day.
Guess what she smells with?
Her feet and antenna.

Can you find all the Critters?